Henry Marcus Leipziger

The Education of the Jews

Henry Marcus Leipziger

The Education of the Jews

ISBN/EAN: 9783337132873

Printed in Europe, USA, Canada, Australia, Japan

Cover: Foto ©ninafisch / pixelio.de

More available books at **www.hansebooks.com**

EDUCATIONAL MONOGRAPHS

PUBLISHED BY THE

NEW YORK COLLEGE FOR THE TRAINING OF TEACHERS

NICHOLAS MURRAY BUTLER, EDITOR

VOL. III. No. 6. } Entered at the Post Office at New York City as second class matter. } WHOLE No. 18.

THE

EDUCATION OF THE JEWS

BY

HENRY M. LEIPZIGER, Ph. D.

Director of the Hebrew Technical Institute, New York.

NEW YORK: 9 UNIVERSITY PLACE
LONDON: THOMAS LAURIE, 28 PATERNOSTER ROW

ISSUED BI-MONTHLY   [$1.00 PER ANNUM.

NOTE.

This monograph is in the main an adaptation of Dr. Samuel Marcus essay entitled "*Zur Schul-Pädagogik des Talmud.*" The works of Güdemann, Strasburger and Simon have, however, been freely consulted.

CONTENTS.

EDUCATION AMONG THE JEWS.

A Study in the History of Pedagogy:

Although education and instruction are co-ordinate, still their methods are somewhat different. The education of a being, as of a nation, begins at birth ; instruction only after a certain degree of intelligence has been attained. Education has for its purpose the improvement of the condition of the human race and the attainment of human perfection. Instruction uses the material that has been handed down to us and that others have found of value in forming and elevating humanity.

Among the wonderful spectacles that the world's history presents, one of the most remarkable is the survival of the Jewish people despite the many vicissitudes it has encountered, and—what is of more interest to the student of education—is the maintenance of the high standard of intellectuality which marks the Hebrew race.

This intellectuality is due to a carefully devised system of training and education—a system without a parallel in the history of nations.

According to Prof. Dittes, "If ever a people has demonstrated the power of education it is the Hebrew people." What is remarkable about the system is that it is adapted to every age and time. No step in the march of progress finds opposition among the Hebrews ; but education is regarded as a process of evolution, a continual becoming.

Education, in a true system, depends upon the ideal that is held up for attainment. What is the perfect man ? In Roman days it was the valiant soldier, capable of enduring fatigue, and stoical as to his fate. Among the Athenians the ideal man was one in whom physical and moral perfection were developed.

As a religion of practical morality Judaism did not create schools of philosophy, but erected schools for children, in which both sexes were trained in the teachings of duty and of love. "Go" said two great heathen thinkers to their contemporaries, " go to the Jewish schools where the children are trained in the observance of the moral law. There is the source of its strength—that is the secret of its indestructibility. If you would conquer them, you must attack these places."

The perfect man among the Hebrews was the virtuous man, the man who strove to be like God. Virtue was placed above everything.

And this ideal colored their system of education. God was their king, their teacher, and their judge, so that Hebrew education was particularly and specially religious. The union was not of church and state, but the more important one of religion and life.

Here, in early times before schools were regularly instituted, the parents were the first teachers. Parents felt an obligation to teach their children as a command of Jehovah, and every possible means was adopted to keep alive a lofty morality and to develop that national pride for God which has marked the Hebrew through all periods of his history.

The celebration of the anniversary of the exodus from Egypt illustrates one means of keeping alive this national

love of God.   On the Passover Evening symbols commem-
orating the great event were explained in each household
to all the family, and the Talmud distinctly advised that
questions should be encouraged.   Even here we see the
application of that pedagogic principle which favors direct
observation and personal reflection as most desirable
among children.   But, strange to say, the contributions of
the Jews to the science of education are but little known.

A study of the history of this race will show that very
many of the new movements in education which mark our
time have been anticipated by them centuries ago.

More than two thousand years ago they recognized the
almost divine office of the teacher, established education for
all upon the most democratic basis, displayed wise pedagogic knowledge in the arrangements of their schools and
course of studies, and at all times favored the education of
the hand in conjunction with the training of the intellect.

In the brief compass of this monograph I can give
but a suggestion of the rich field that the student of peda-
gogy will find in the history of the Hebrew people.
Certainly in the development of an American ideal, much
can be learned from studying the methods which have won
for the Hebrew race the following characterization:
"Israel had a higher part assigned her in the drama of
history, to which her secret instincts resistlessly drew her.
Her predominant characteristic was an intense religious-
ness.   Everything in the life of her people took on a
serious and devout tone.   Patriotism was identified with
piety.   Her statesmen were reformers, idealists, whose
orations were sermons like the speeches of Gladstone in
the Midlothian campaign, dealing with politics in the
light of eternal principles. * * * The nation's ambitions
were aspirations. Her heroes grew to be saints. The divine
became to her not the true or the beautiful, but the good.
She evidently had, as Matthew Arnold said of John
Wesley, " a genius for godliness."

The character of Hebrew education during the Biblical period will be but briefly considered. The main portion of the essay will however be devoted to a view of Jewish theories and methods during the Talmudic times, which extend from Ezra's time until about the 5th century of the present era.

The Rabbis claim that systematic instruction dates from a very early period, but give no particulars as to the school. It is clear, though, from frequent references in the Bible, that all education was given at home—the parents being the first teachers. The child was not trained to be skilful in the use of weapons, or to become an artist, but a firm believer in God ; so that as soon as he could talk his lips whispered of God.

The laws of Moses require the fathers to " speak of Him when thou sittest in thy house, and when thou goest in thy way, and when thou sittest down, and when thou risest up."

That the higher classes at this time were cultured is admitted, but it seems certain, from the learning of men like Amos and Michah, that ability to read and write—as yet an unattained ideal among many peoples—was general. In the course of time there arose a class of men called Sopherim or Scribes who gradually supplanted the power of the priesthood, and who became the forerunners of the great Talmudic teachers.

In Samuel's time the schools of the Prophets came into existence. Some consider these schools as the originators of the cloister, others the first academies. In these schools religion, poetry and music were taught.

The first years of childhood were spent under the mother's care, later on the father took care of his son. Ethics was the staple of instruction. Short aphorisms were repeated by the young pupil and much instruction was conveyed in the form of parables and riddles. Religious observances exercised a great educational influence.

The ceremonial law, was so thoroughly interspersed with so many holy and wise teachings that it was a complete manual of study. Nor were natural phenomena permitted to occur without being brought into play in their system of religious training.

A prominent characteristic of the teaching at this period was the answering of children's questions. One comes constantly across passages as follows: "If your son should ask you the reason of this or that law or custom, then explain to him. Wait till a suitable opportunity occurs. Do not rest satisfied with the mere dry statement of the fact but let the practice precede the instruction and then will the law become his possession."

As soon as the child reached his third year he began to memorize verses from the Bible, and when old enough a tablet was given on which he learned to form the letters. At table the children were arranged in the order of their age, so that the older children exercised dominion over the younger.

The foundation of a system of schools among the Jews may be attributed to Simon ben Shetach, who lived 80 B. C. He felt the force of what Fichte afterwards said, "Whatever you would put in a nation's life you must put into its schools," and he enunciated the proposition— not yet universally assented to—that popular education is the best strength of a nation.

Troublous times occurred in Judea. The Holy City resounded with the tramp of the Roman soldier and the Temple was in ruins. Then Jochanan ben Sakkai obtained from the Roman Emperor Titus the privilege of establishing a school at Jamnia. And from this little spark the fire of education was enkindled—a fire which has steadily burnt among the Jewish people even until our day. During the period from the destruction of the Second Temple until about 500 of this era, the Talmud was in process of growth.

The Babylonian Talmud was for more than a thousand years the very essence of spiritual and intellectual activity of the Jews. Its very existence is an evidence of the influence of the schools. This wonderful work—this unique monument of lore—has been much misunderstood. "It is not a text book or a law book; it is a veritable encyclopedia."

Its influence on the Jewish people has been described as follows :

" The historical accounts contained in the Talmud fill a chasm in the history of the Jews and Judaism for which we might, else, in vain seek the bridge.

The Talmud, containing the literature of the Jews, and alluding to so many sciences, and requiring for its understanding several preparatory sciences and other acquirements, set an example and excited the Jews of the middle ages to literary pursuits, and thus gave rise to numbers of works, the variety and ingenuity of which extort, not unfrequently, marks of acknowledgment, even from the bitterest enemies of Judaism, and prevented the Jews from falling into the same ignorance which prevailed through centuries among European Christians. To the discipline of Talmudic study, requiring, as it does, such acuteness of perception and such subtlety of reasoning, may be attributed the success with which the Jews have, in all ages been enabled to extricate themselves from the snares and pitfalls which might else have been their destruction. Moreover, in those unhappy times when the Jews were compelled to live secluded from the rest of mankind, their spirit would have become entirely torpid for want of exercise, had the Talmud not kept alive their faculties, by offering to them so vast a field of mental exercise. Lastly, by rendering the Jews a literary nation, and by having thus continually sharpened and exercised their mental faculties, the Talmud made the possibility (nay, accounted for the fact) that in much less than a century, during which

the barriers have been struck down which excluded the
Jews from the remainder of European society, they have
exhibited a flexibility of intellect, which both in art and
science, produced so many great minds, as to exceed by
far all expectation."

And of this book, the great scholar Delitzsch says:

"The Talmud, that colossal Jewish religious code, in
which the Jew, educated in the lore of his nation, finds his
spiritual house, is to the educated in Christendom less
known than the Vedas of the Indians or the Avesta of
the Persians."

The Proverbs of Solomon contain sentences on education which were not for an age but " for all time ;" while
in the apocryphal book of Sirach we find a " book rich
in pedagogical insight, which paints with master-strokes
the relations of husband and wife, parents and children,
master and servant, friend and friend, enemy and enemy,
and the dignity of labor as well as its division. This price-
less book forms a side-piece to the Republic of Plato and
his laws on ethical government."

We are not surprised that a race that had made two
such contributions to educational literature should in the
Talmud evolve a perfect pedagogic system. In its pages
will be found gems of educational wisdom. At a time
when the schoolmaster was despised, when intellectual
darkness reigned in all the European countries, the Jewish
rabbis carefully elaborated and practiced those wise pedagogic rules which are to-day slowly but surely coming in
vogue. Only within the present generation has England
established a national elementary school system. The
Jews established theirs twenty centuries ago. The Puritan
fathers only carried into practice sound Jewish teaching
when they insisted with Joshua ben Gamala that every
community should support a school. Truly it can be
said in the words of Isaiah, "Out of Zion shall go
forth the law, and the word of the Lord from Jerusalem."

We shall consider the subject under the following heads.
I.   Importance of Schools and Instruction.
II. Founding and Spread of Schools.
III. School Organization—including
    A.   School house.
    B.   Teachers.
    C.   Schools.
    D.   Material.
    E.   Method.
    F.   Regulations.

IMPORTANCE OF SCHOOLS AND INSTRUCTION.

The wise men of the Talmudic times had the highest conception of the value of schools and instruction; the school was to them the long and short of life. The profession of teaching was regarded as the very highest, as one in which God himself was engaged. "What does God do in the fourth hour?" is once asked in the Talmud. "He teaches little school children." The ancient history of other nations may be searched in vain for a single instance of regard of the high importance of the school, such as Rabbi Jehuda uttered in such distinct words when he said "The world is only saved by the breath of the school children."

The importance of the school and instruction, according to the Talmud, cannot be overrated. The very stability of the world, if it is to be the abode of intelligent beings, is connected with the school as effect is to cause.

"A city without schools should be destroyed or excommunicated." And "Jerusalem was destroyed because its people neglected the schools and school children."

As a consequence, the teachers and schools were regarded as the keepers and defenders of the city. For where spirituality dwells in a people or state, which permits all circles of life, there the moral perfection of all its citizens is striven after, and the teachers of children take an honored place in society, and become the real defenders of the city ; educating, training and elevating its citizens. " A President of the Academy " relates the Talmud "once sent several learned men from Palestine to aid the progress of instruction and establish schools where none existed. They came to a city where they saw no sign of a school nor could they find a teacher. They said to the citizens, ' bring the keepers of the city before us.' The magistrate and the chief police officials appeared. 'These are not the city's keepers !' the wise men exclaimed. ' Who then are ? ' asked the citizens in astonishment. ' The city's keepers are the teachers,' was the reply."

" When you see lovely gardens by the stream and the brilliant stars in heaven," says the Talmud, "then you have a picture of the true teacher, who takes care of the tender plants and sheds mild light on the dark world of growing childhood." The most beautiful ornaments of humanity are the teachers surrounded by children.

This conception arose from a natural feeling of *love* which they fostered. Each teacher felt it to be the most welcome task of his life to teach. The Talmud relates of Jochanan ben Sakkai that he spent a third of his life in teaching, and the Rabbi Akiba said to one of his disciples, "My, son, the cow is more anxious to suckle than the calf to suck."

The classic nations of antiquity did not have the same regard for the dignity of the teacher as the Jews did. Among the Greeks and Romans the trainer of children was a man without standing, a veritable pariah in the community. The post of teacher was despised, and the teacher and servant were put on par.

This is what Plutarch says of the Roman pedagogue : " For if any of their servants be better than the rest, they dispose some of them to follow husbandry, some to navigation, some to merchandise, some to be stewards in their houses, and some lastly to put out their money to use for them. But if they find any slave that is a drunkard or a glutton, and unfit for any other business, to him they assign the government of their children ; whereas, a good pedagogue ought to be such a one in his disposition as Phœnix, tutor to Achilles was."

The life of the teacher was closely bound to that of the scholar. Teacher and scholar were one and inseparable. Teachers and scholars shared each other's failures.

The disinterestedness with which they pursued their vocation indicates the love they had for their calling. The only reward which they were promised and which they desired, was to learn and then to teach. He who studies the law in his youth will use it in old age. He who has pupils in his youth will have them when he is old.

The father was no less convinced of the importance of instruction to the child. "A learned man," says the Talmud, "met a friend leading his son hurriedly to school."

"Why such haste" he asked him.

"Because," he replied, "the duty to lead the child to instruction precedes all other cares."

Another learned man did not eat his morning meal before his son was in school.

The esteem for the teacher and the love for him made instruction thus a pleasant duty.

Relating to teachers the Talmud says :

"He who has studied and does not teach resembles a myrtle in the desert."

But it was not the teacher alone who strove to awaken the intelligence of the child and to guide it in the right path ; the father was obliged to do his share. "Who is ignorant? He who has sons and does not have them taught."

Many are the aphorisms to be found in the pages of the

Talmud on the importance of industry and perseverance
in study. "The day is short and the work great, the
workers are lazy, the reward is great, and the Master
praises." "It is not the same if one studies alone or with
a teacher." "Do not say 'When I get time, I will study.'
Perhaps you will not get time."

RISE AND SPREAD OF SCHOOLS.

It is to Joshua ben Gamala that the organization of the
Jewish school system is due. More then eighteen centuries ago he initiated it, carefully nursed it, and planted
the seed so thoroughly that even in the smallest village a
school became recognized as a necessity. It was he who
thus started that intellectual movement which has characterized the Jewish people down to the present day.

"Before Joshua ben Gamala," relates the Talmud, "the
father was the teacher of his children—and fatherless
children received no instruction. To supply the need,
children's schools were established in Jerusalem."

But things went on as before and only children who had
fathers to look after them attended these schools, while
the fatherless and uncared-for child as a rule did not go to
school.

Then a school was established in each community, which
was attended by scholars who had reached sixteen years
of age, who did not need the discipline of the child
and were left at their option. It was then that Joshua ben
Gamala appeared and ordered that in each town a school
should be established and that children from the age of
six upwards should be obliged to attend thereat.

From that time on, school instruction was a matter
conducted in real earnestness, as the ordinances established
sufficiently prove. After Rabbi Joshua's law was promul-
gated no one was permitted to take a child to school

from one city to another, the inhabitants of each city could
be forced to maintain schools and teachers, and there was
a stern prohibition against living in a town which was not
provided with a school.

Rabbi Joshua's work was not temporary. Its effect was
lasting. The spread of schools during his time was the
most extensive that we can imagine. Schools sprung up
everywhere and parents cheerfully brought their children
to them. And if, perhaps, some of the Talmudic statements
in reference to the number of schools, scholars and teachers
appear at times exaggerated, still the fact remains
that in every important city the school attendance was
very great.

INNER ORGANIZATION OF THE SCHOOLS.

A. SCHOOLROOMS.

Space, Name, and Arrangement.

At the beginning of the Talmudic period it was the custom, in case no proper house was provided, to give instruction in some place in the open air. But from the time of
Rabbi Jehuda Hanassi instruction was given in rooms
specially arranged. These schools went under various
names, such as Beth Hamedrath (House of Learning),
Yeshiba (and sometimes under the Greek name "Skole),"
Schools for children were held in what were termed Beth
Ha-Keneseth. They were generally situated in the
quieter parts of the city, so that the lessons might not
be disturbed. Benches, stools, and cushions were only
introduced into schools long after the schools themselves
were established.

Maimonides furnishes a very correct picture of a school
in practical operation.

" The teacher sat above, and the scholars surrounded him

as a crown the head, so that all could see and hear the teacher. The teacher did not sit on a chair while his scholars sat on the floor, but *all* sat either upon chairs or upon the floor. It was formerly the custom for the teacher to sit while the scholars stood, but shortly before the destruction of Jerusalem it was arranged that both scholars and teachers should sit. Children sat *in front* of their teacher so that they could see his face when he spoke, in accordance with the words of Isaiah 30 : 20, "Thine eyes shall see thy teacher."

The school houses were the favorites of the Jewish people. There they were wont to assemble. The house, the school and the synagogue formed a three-fold link which bound the race of the old book to the book of the ancient race. The school house was open all day.

B. THE TEACHER.

(a). *Choice of Teachers.*

On moral grounds no unmarried man or any woman could be a teacher. And among the number of those eligible to teachership only the best were chosen. The words of Rabbi Akiba are noteworthy in this regard. " Do you desire to hang yourself? If so, select a lofty tree," which, interpreted, means, " Learn from a distinguished teacher." The most experienced teacher was regarded as the most desirable, and when it came to a choice, always had the preference. " Instruction by young teacher " says the Talmud " is like sour grapes and new wine, while instruction by old teachers is like ripe grapes and sweet wine."

If however a less capable teacher had once been engaged, he was not set aside for a more competent, and for this reason. Perhaps the latter would be careless, since he would boast that he had no peer, and would not fear dismissal. The Talmud gives many "points" that should be considered in selecting teachers. In one place the teacher who gives his pupils much matter although he does not ground them in it is preferred, while in another· place *thoroughness* is deemed most desirable. On the whole *thoroughness* was the chief point desired, because the Talmud lays great stress on the development of the understanding and the memory, and thoroughness is a great aid thereto.

(*b*). *Qualifications of the Teacher.*

Even temper and calmness, which do not permit of sudden anger, patience so that the teacher enters into the environment of the child and thinks with him,—these are the chief qualifications of the teacher. So Hillel said, " A hot-tempered man cannot be a teacher."

The Talmud says that " No child can ask too many questions from his teacher ; he must repeat again and again so that he shall thoroughly understand what has been taught."

As additional qualifications, truth and exactness were demanded from the teacher. So highly impressed were the Talmudists with the sacredness of the teacher's work— for it is none other than humanizing the world—that school instruction was styled "God's work," so that according to Maimonides a careless teacher received the following severe criticism : " The teacher who permits his pupils to remain idle, or engage in other work during school time, or is careless about his instruction, belongs to those of whom it is said 'Cursed be those who manage the work of God basely.'"

Piety and culture are finally the indispensable requirements of a teacher.

(*c*). *Respect for the Teacher.*

Owing to the esteem with which instruction was regarded and to the responsibility placed upon the teacher,. a deep respect for the teaching profession followed as a matter

of course, for the teacher was considered as the expounder
of the truth and the founder of human morals and well-
being. Among the ancient Hebrews respect for teachers
was identical with respect for God and his law. "Respect
your teacher as you would God." Irreverence towards
teachers was severely punished, and it was said that
"Jerusalem was destroyed because the teachers of that city
were deposed."

Teachers were even more respected than parents. "The
teacher precedes the father ; the wise man, the King." If
the father and teacher are both a prisoner, we should first
free the teacher, then the father, for the one gives him only
the temporary, the other eternal life.

A few examples of reverence, although intended more
for advanced student schools, are still characteristic.

The scholar must not express his opinion in religious
or ceremonial subjects in the presence of his teacher.

He must not walk at the right of his teacher.

He must not call his teacher by name.

He must not sit in his chair, nor pray before him nor
behind his back, he must not go to bathe with him, he
must not contradict him in his presence, etc.

All services that a servant must do for his master must
a scholar do for his teacher except to take off and put on
his shoes, etc.

When a scholar leaves his teacher's presence, he must
not turn his face from him but gradually turn from him.

C. THE PUPIL.

(a). *School-Age.*

Recognizing the fact that systematic instruction before
the sixth year would injure the bodily development of
children and because they wished to foster a sound mind

in a sound body, the wise men of the Talmud fixed upon the sixth year as the time for going to school. "He who sends his son to school before his sixth year runs after him and cannot catch him;" and this is interpreted to mean he wants to strengthen and maintain him and cannot, because the boy is doomed to die on account of weakness.

Still children were early taught the elements of religion. "As soon as the child begins to speak" reads an old precept, "shall the father teach it the confession of God's unity. 'Hear, O Israel, the Lord our God is one Lord.'"

(b). *The Psychical Individuality of the Pupil.*

As attention was paid to the pupil's physical development, so too was his psychical individuality cared for. He was not rapidly hurried from one subject to another, but led slowly and according to his ability to comprehend and grasp it. The subjects of instruction were adapted to the age and mental ability of the pupil. Until the tenth year Biblical instruction was the chief study, so that at ten years of age the pupil was thoroughly conversant with the Bible. From his tenth year upwards, the Mishna and Gemara (divisions of the Talmud) were the special topics of instruction. With increasing mental power, subjects of corresponding difficulty were introduced into the school curriculum.

It is not always the case that as a child grows older his mental grasp is strengthened, and therefore it is advised that while at the beginning of instruction, when the mind is still free, great attention should be paid, because what is learnt as a child remains in the memory like ink written on clean paper ; still if the child does not progress, great forebearance should be exercised with him until his twelfth year. From that time he should be severely disciplined because about the twelfth year the normal child attains possession of his mental powers.

The ability to comprehend a subject and the love for study appears in different children at different periods of

their lives. Some children readily remember and understand all that the teacher tells them. Some however
understand readily but do not remember. Others again
recollect the illustrations which a teacher uses but do not
understand the subject at all, and some are just the opposite.
These four classes of pupils are thus characterized in the
Mishna. "There are four kinds of scholars ; a sponge, a
funnel, a sieve, a winnow. The sponge absorbs everything, the funnel takes all in at one end and lets it out at
the other, the sieve lets the wine pass through and keeps
the lees, and the winnow removes the coarse meal and
keeps the fine."

These characterizations furnish a key to the manage-
ment of the various subjects of instruction, namely, that
the teacher must use a different method in dealing with
the different categories of pupils. With pupils of the first
and last classes the instruction can be broader and illus-
trated from collateral subjects, while with the other two
classes it is recommended to stick close to the topic and
to use simplest illustrations. Similar advice is given to
teachers with regard to the varying memory stages of the
pupil. Four qualities make their appearance among
pupils : Some understand readily and forget quickly ; here
the advantage balances the disadvantage. Some grasp
slowly and forget slowly. In this case the disadvantage
balances the advantage. Some grasp quickly and forget
slowly—that is a good quality ; and finally some learn
slowly and forget quickly—that is a bad trait. The teacher
can by various means overcome these difficulties—nor
will he complain about them, for these very weaknesses
compel him to think about ways and means of removing
them.

It was recognized that learning, in a narrow sense,
depends upon the activity of the memory as a preparation
for the other mental powers. Great stress was therefore
laid on the cultivation of the memory and it almost became

axiomatic that " Knowledge is won by aid of recollection, therefore train the memory." The development of the memory was attained in the following ways.

1. By practice, which was constant and gradual.
2. By discipline.
3. By thorough preparation of the subject.

(c). *Behavior of the Pupil.*

As Socrates did not accept as his pupil every one who applied to him but like his predecessor Pythagoras was affected by the outward appearance and demeanor of the scholar, so too did the Talmudic teachers in their high schools. Rabbi Gamaliel said, "every scholar whose deportment does not correspond to his inner aspirations should not attend the house of instruction." The same idea prevailed in elementary schools. As soon as a child proved himself incorrigible and liable to exert a baneful influence on his fellow pupils he was removed. " He who permits an unworthy pupil to remain in the school must be responsible for the evil consequences."

(d). *Honor of the Pupil.*

"Think as much of your pupil's honor as of your own ;" so reads a direction of the Talmud to teachers and educators in regard to the fostering of the feeling of honor in the child. This precept is of great pedagogic value, because if it is followed the foundation of a lofty feeling of honor will be early laid in the child. In every child there is feeling of self respect which is his dearest possession. This feeling evidences itself in many ways in the school room—perhaps as a keen appetite for study and a desire to be the head of the class, or in an endeavor to be the most modest and industrious pupil.

The cultivation of this feeling, then, becomes one of the most important duties of the teacher, and he was warned against hurting, particularly in any public way, the feelings of his pupil.

D. SUBJECTS OF INSTRUCTION.

(a). *National Literature.*

The subjects of instruction may be generally classed under the head, national literature, which includes the religious writings—the Bible and the Talmud. These subjects were so arranged that their study, as we shall see, covered nearly all known sciences.

The course of study was divided into three parts, 1st, Mikra (reading) ; 2nd, Mishna (repetition of the law) ; 3d, Gemara, (completion). The primary classes studied Mikra, and, according to Maimonides, the school session lasted all day. This may appear strange to us. It is probable that games were interspersed in the hours of instruction, and from time to time the teacher varied the exercises by relating parables or legends from the Talmud. (Hagada.)

The second division studied Mishna. Here the pupils ranged from 10 to 15 years. The teacher explained the oral law, or laws interpreting or explaining the Mosaic law, and which was put in form by Rabbi Judahin in the third century. Most of the instruction was oral.

The students from 15 to 18 years of age studied the Gemara. The oral laws form the subject of discussion and the students criticize the interpretations freely yet respectfully, and contrast two *Halachoth* (Rules). The teacher's duty is to refute the students' objections.

The various discussions embrace in their course natural history, anatomy, medicine, geometry and astronomy, all of which sciences were considered however only as the periphery of the true science, which was the law.

As soon as the child was able to read, the teacher began instruction in the Bible, and certain particular passages were preferred. The portions chosen for the beginning were either the 3d Book of Moses—containing the law for the priests, or the directions as to sacrifices. "Why," asked the wise men "should the first instruction in the Bible to children begin with the laws about sacrifices?" "Because little children are innocent and pure, and sacrifices are symbols of purity."

In the higher schools instruction ·was given in Talmudic subjects. The Gemara was only taught in the most advanced schools.

(b). *Foreign Languages.*

There are many facts to prove that in Talmudic times the Jews were well acquainted with foreign tongues; thus we find the query as to whether law could be read in distant lands in the language of the country.

Great value was attached to the study of languages ·as is shown by these remarkable words: "Holy Scripture says that God not only created heaven and earth but also language—because language creates a new world, the world of thought." All languages, even those of Israel's oppressors, were considered of great importance. Of all tongues, the Greek language was the favorite foreign speech of the Jews. "The law may be translated only into the Greek tongue because only that language can fully interpret it."

The Jews were always lovers of the beautiful and noble and the richness and pleasant sound of Greek particularly attracted them. Greek was considered the proper language for poetry. "Four languages," it is said, "which were spoken in and about Palestine possess each distinct attributes. Greek sounds sweet on account of its rhythm in song; Latin, on account of its sonorousness in battle; Syriac, by reason of its numerous voices in songs of lamentation and Hebrew on account of its distinctness in speaking." Instruction in Greek was general. This love for the Greek tongue remained for centuries among the

Jews. The President of the Academy in Nahardea was skilled both in Hebrew and Greek lore. In Spain, in Saragossa and Barcelona, Greek was earnestly studied, so much so that in the year 1304 the Jews of Spain felt obliged to forbid the learning of Greek before the 25th year. Although the Jews showed such a decided preference for Greek culture, still it did not prevent them from taking an interest in the languages and sciences suited to their time.

As in Palestine during the period of the second temple, the Hebrew tongue was gradually replaced by a Syriac idiom spoken by the neighboring peoples; as in Alexandria the Jews spoke and wrote Greek, so at the time of the destruction of the second temple the Jews appear as Latin poets and critics. Unprejudiced and willing, they went about their work, encouraged by their words. "Every word that proceeds from God's mouth is divided into seventy parts—i.e., into all the languages of the world;" meaning that no matter in what tongue an idea was expressed, it became a power for good, provided it was true and liberal.

(c). *Astronomy, Mathematics and Natural Sciences.*

The life of the old Hebrew was dedicated to the pursuit of religion; so the study of these sciences was not merely for intellectual purposes, nor for information that might lead to man's advantage or give him a loftier idea of the glory of God, but solely as an aid and help to religion. They were used as means for a deeper study of the law which formed to them the center of a circle as the sciences formed the periphery.

Many passages from the Talmud prove that these sciences were studied at this period. Rabbi Gamliel had in his study, charts and pictures of the moon. Samuel, a noted Rabbi, said he was as much at home in the streets of the heavens as he was in the streets of Nahardea.

Many of the Tractates of the Talmud show an extensive acquaintance with geometry. In another tractate a long list of plants and animals can be found. Still another furnishes information concerning animal anatomy.

It is doubtful whether these subjects were regularly taught in the elementary schools, but it is certain that the pupils of maturer age advanced far beyond the mere elements of these sciences.

(*d*). *Gymnastics*.

Gymnastics seems to have formed a part of divine worship in Mosaic times. It appears from the Bible that in David's days games with weapons and other forms of athletic skill were general. In Talmudic times the development of the body was advocated, partly as a personal benefit, partly also on religious grounds. This is shown by the command : "Every father must have his child taught to swim."

In the time of Antiochus Epiphanes, Greek gymnastics were introduced into Palestine, and the Hellenic party built a gymnasium in Jerusalem. At the time of the Roman rule in Judea, there were Roman circuses in many towns of Palestine, against visiting which Rabbi Meir warned the Jews, as destined to lead them to worship Roman gods.

But both intellectual and physical culture were considered only as accessories in Hebrew education, that which formed the principles of their teaching was morality and religion. So it was that, quite different from the old Spartans, physical deformity was not considered a crime in Hebrew eyes ; and never were they guilty of that exposing of children which forms such a blot on the record of so many nations of antiquity. That, however, which they did regard with horror, and which they punished severely, was moral deformity, which might prevent the child from becoming an honest and moral man.

E. METHOD.

(a). *The Outward Bearing of the Teacher.*

In order to arouse the scholar's interest in his studies the Talmud deemed it necessary that between pupil and teacher feelings of mutual regard should exist. This should be brought about by the teacher encouraging the youthful tendency to cheerfulness, without however degenerating into frivolity. A distinguished teacher, relates the Talmud, awakened the interest of his pupils by beginning his lectures with a humorous anecdote, and then proceeded to the subject in hand, to which the scholars gave most earnest attention.

This cheerful earnestness should mark all intercourse between pupil and teacher. It is highly important that the teacher should listen patiently to the many questions of the learner so that he may ward off that sense of false shame which hinders so many children in their pursuit of knowledge.

(b). *Knowing and Understanding.*

In the earliest stages of education, the Talmudists advised that children first be furnished with subject matter before they are ready for reflecting thereupon. "First learn and then apprehend." For this reason it was forbidden to give the children opportunity for unnecessary investigation of things. "Take your children away from unnecessary reflection."

Even for adults this rule held good, and therefore the endeavor of all was for knowing to precede apprehension.

(c). *Memory Exercise.*

While it is advised that in the beginning acquaintance with the subject matter should be the main point aimed at, still it was not meant that the instruction should be mechanical. On the contrary means were given to the teacher by which he should stimulate the thinking faculty and awaken the power of observation. Teachers were recommended to ask odd and queer questions in order to startle and then to concentrate the attention on the very opposite.

(d). *Form of Imparting Instruction.*

The subjects of instruction were divided into portions which had to be studied in a definite period. These periods were five years each and these were again subdivided into yearly periods, in order to render it possible for the pupils to grasp the entire subject. The existence of this plan shows that a *successive* method was employed. Instruction in the Bible and the Talmud did not go hand in hand, but the one followed the other; this being the principle, "If you lay hold of too much at once you get hold of nothing."

In order to aid the pupil's understanding, the teacher should not give too much matter at once, but give a little at a time and allow a period of rest. "God himself did not give Moses the Law all at once, but revealed it to him in several periods. How much more should this be done in human instruction."

Brevity is particularly recommended. The teacher should be sparing of his words, and express himself in the concisest manner possible. Learned digressions from the subject should be avoided and scholars should not be told in three words what could be said in one. "Always teach your pupils in the shortest possible manner."

(e). *Thoroughness in Instruction.*

The choice of the shortest method of instruction aids thoroughness, since too much can more readily injure than too little.

As means towards *thoroughness* the Talmud advises (1) careful and correct grounding, and (2) *practice* and *repetition.* Rabbi Akiba said, "The teacher must not only make the lesson clear to his pupils by means of illustrations and explanations, but must be untiring until they thoroughly grasp the contents of what he has taught." One Rabbi repeated a certain matter four hundred times to one of his scholars before he fully comprehended it.

Such methods were used (1) to prevent superficiality in learning, (2) to impress the knowledge acquired upon the memory, (3) to promote the acquisition of further knowledge.

The latter two points were stimulated by *viva voce* repetition of the pupil, and a system of mnemonics. (*a*) Vocal repetition of the learner fixes the matter in the memory. "Open your eyes" says the Talmud " so that you may keep your knowledge, and that it may be alive in you." (*b*) The old Greeks treasured and practiced an art of memory which was based on the law of association. The Jews, too, valued the system of mnemonics as a valuable help to memory. They used certain "catchwords" having sounds or letters which would remind them of the contents of the paragraph, or they used well known quotations from the Bible or Proverbs, or names of well known persons or places.

(*f*). *Other Methods.*

In order to sharpen the child's intellect it was considered advisable to change the school it attended in order that it might get the benefit of a new method or of greater ability in teaching. "Children should be taken from one school to another so that they may learn from the teachers who perhaps may have greater ability to give instruction." "He who learns constantly from the same teacher and gets only his opinion of the law, sees no sign of the blessing." "A scholar who finds difficulty in learning should visit several schools."

Older pupils were advised to study in groups without reference to the fact whether both were equally studious. As a little piece of wood can light a large piece, so the young and less capable pupils stimulate the large and more developed ones. Iron sharpens iron, i.e., as one piece of iron sharpens another so one scholar does the other.

Disputation in debate is a most valuable aid to thoroughness, therefore the Talmud declares "Knowledge becomes the property of the student by disputation, and elaborating the phrase" *docendo discimus*, Rabbi Chanina said "I have learnt much from my teacher, more from my fellow students, most of all from my scholars."

(g). *Connection between Instruction and Life.*

While the Jews believed in education for education's sake, still they regarded the theoretical side of instruction but as a preparation for practical life. The saying "Not learning but doing is the principal thing," is proof that the school was not the end in itself, but only a means and a preparation for life and thus they evinced in their way their belief in the principle, "Non scholae sed vitae discimus."

The practice of the Law is more important than the study. He who knows the theory but never practices is an *am haarez* (ignoramus). Practice was acquired in association with learned men or teachers. This was considered very valuable, since the ordinary conversation of wise men is profitable.

Without regard to social position in life, the Talmud ordered that, besides study, a handicraft should be learned. "As it is your duty to teach your son the law teach him a trade." "Disobedience to this ordinance exposes one to just contempt, for thereby the social condition of all was endangered." "He who does not have his son taught a trade prepares him to be a robber." "He who applies himself to study alone, is like him who has no God."

For the before-mentioned reasons ·and because one-sidedness in education was undesirable and partly for hygienic reasons, the greatest teachers of the Talmudic period were also workmen, who, while pulling the thread through the sole of the shoe or rolling their barrels to the market place, were meditating upon serious philosophical questions.

(h). *Influence of Instruction on Piety and Morality.*

The old Jews did not aim at intellectual progress only, but their principal endeavor was to develop the moral and spiritual side of man. Their endeavors were directed therefore not alone toward knowledge, but also toward love and reverence of God, and the development of the moral. feeling and will. To think honestly and to act honestly must be the result of the study of the law. Abaji taught, it is said, "Thou shalt love the Eternal, thy God;" that means that, through you, God's name shall become beloved and glorified.

Thou shalt learn and mix with wise men, but all thy acts must be honest and thy words gentle, so that the people will say "Hail! to him, because he has studied the law; hail! his father, who permitted him to study; hail! his teacher, who taught him; woe to those who have learnt nothing! Look at him who has studied, how pleasant are his ways and how gracious his deeds!" But if you have studied and mixed with the wise, and your conduct toward your fellow men is not seemly, then will the people say, "Woe to him who has studied! woe to his father who had him instructed! woe to his teacher who has taught him! Look at him who has studied the law how corrupt are his acts and how hateful are his ways!"

The child must learn as early as possible to avoid pride
and honestly to direct his better mind to study ; to show
respect for his teacher, his superior, respect for all from
whom he receives instruction, and above all respect for the
elders, to imitate whom he must constantly strive.

"Only he possesses true knowledge who does not display
it." "The law is not in heaven, where you must ascend, or
on the other side of the sea," i.e., you will find it neither with
him who in the extent of his thoughts resembles the ocean;
nor will you find it among the proud or around merchants
or pedlars; "Why," it is said in another place, "does
the Book of the Law resemble water? For it is said 'Come
ye that are thirsty, drink!'" Because the law, like the
water which leaves its high position and chooses a lower
spot for its slopping, has its seat among the humble in
spirit. Another Rabbi asked, "Why does the scripture
resemble water, wine and milk?" Because as these three
drinks are kept in ordinary vessels, so are also the words
of the law only in meek men."

The following story illustrates the point. The daughter
of a Roman Emperor once asked Rabbi Joshua ben Chan-
aujah, how it was that so gifted a man as he was so ugly.
Without replying to her question he asked her, " In what
kind of vessels are your father's finest wine kept?" " In
earthen ones" she replies. " I am surprised at that" he
said. "Wine for the royal table should be kept in gold-
en vessels." And she told her father the Rabbi's opinion,
and he had gold and silver vessels made for the purpose.
But the wine turned sour. When the Emperor asked
Rabbi Joshua his advice on this subject, he said his words
were only a reply to his daughter's question.

SCHOOL REGULATIONS.
(a). *Classes.*

The perfection of school organization is attained when
the scholars are arranged according to their mental stature

and where each class is provided with proper instruction. In the Talmudic schools there were such divisions. The Beth Hamidrash or house of study was divided, as we have before said, into three great departments, each of which covered a course of five years, and each course was sub-divided in smaller courses, graded into lower and higher degrees. It was not possible for the same teacher to give instruction to a beginner and one who had already attended school for some time. In many of the classes there were monitors, generally the best scholar. He received his instruction with the rest of his classmates and then imparted his knowledge to the weaker pupils. The teacher was thus not hindered by the weaker pupils and they enjoyed the benefit of extra instruction. The pupils were accustomed to be seated, according to their rank, and the desire to be head of the class was certainly a great stimulus. In many of the classes too, instruction was given by a teacher who had a special knowledge either of the Bible or the Mishna or the Gemara.

(b). Number of Scholars in a Class.

How many children can a teacher, with advantage, instruct ? In our day when classes often contain more than sixty children, the teacher's duty seems to consist in get-ting "around the class once." The Talmud says "For one teacher there should be twenty-five scholars ; If there are fifty, there should be two teachers. If there are forty an assistant teacher should be appointed, and these teachers should be paid by the city." It may have been that these rules were adopted for sanitary reasons, for in a crowded room the vitiated atmosphere affects the physical condition of the children. Or perhaps too many children in a class make it difficult for the teacher to properly per-form his functions. The maximum of scholars for one teacher was fixed at twenty-five, for double that number there were two parallel classes each with a regular teacher. If the number of scholars was not sufficient however for the employment of an extra teacher the brighter scholars were called in to help. Both Bell and Lancaster adopted this monitorial system, although in Talmudic days it was not abused.

(c). *School Sessions.*

Punctuality in coming and going, in beginning and ending, is of great advantage in instruction. A fixed time for opening and closing the school. Instruction was commenced very early in the morning. According to Maimonides, the school period continued without interruption, and instruction was given every day in the week and all day long with the exception of a recess mid-day. The only holidays were the sabbaths and festivals. The interruption of school instruction was strictly prohibited. Nothing was important enough to supplant it. The Talmud says " The instruction of children may not be interrupted even on account of the building of the Temple." It may seem in our time impossible or unwise to continue the school session the whole year, but there is a tendency even in our time to use the vacations to the pupil's advantage by the study of nature, and by kindred means.

(d). *School Rules.*

The following are some of the Talmudic school rules :

a. Punctuality and regularity in attendance at school.

b. Pupils to be arranged according to their class standing.

c. No pupil was permitted to leave his seat without permission.

d. The scholar was not permitted to question the teacher immediately upon his entrance into the school room.

e. Questions not pertaining to the subject matter of instruction must not be asked.

f. Two scholars were not permitted to ask questions at the same time.

(*e*). *School Punishments and Rewards.*

The old Hebrews appealed in these respects more to the feeling than to the reason. He who gives instruction either to large or small pupils should not compel them to study by threats, or chastisement. The teacher should rather win the heart of the pupil, without however becoming too familiar with him. There should always exist on the part of the scholars a degree of reverence for the teacher. This advice is given to teachers, "Occasionally be very strict, without however being harsh." The Talmud says "Push away with your left hand, but bring back again with your right ; and do not do like the prophet Elisha, who pushed away his servant Gehazi with both hands and made him an apostate from his people." And again, "Pupils should be punished with one hand and caressed with two." This mild discipline was always effective when it appealed to the sense of honor of the pupil. In the case of small children, where the feeling is not yet developed, the Talmud recommends light corporal punishment and a deprivation of food. The grown up pupil however must not be punished corporally. In administering punishment the individuality of children should be considered. It thus can happen that two children guilty of the same offence would be punished in different ways ; or even one child should receive punishment and the other be sufficiently punished by the dread of it. If bodily punishment was given it was very light. The teacher was not permitted to hit with a stick for it might easily wound, but used a shoe-string instead.. As punishment is a part of school discipline, so also is reward. It is said that one distinguished

Rabbi had in his elementary school, honey which he gave as a reward to the children. In the reward and the treatment of children there was one main rule of discipline and that was the equality of all children before the teacher. Therefore the Talmud disapproves of the conduct of Jacob in preferring Joseph to his brothers, and regards that as one of the reasons for the bondage in Egypt.

(*f*). *School Dues.*

The old Hebrews believed in the principle enunciated by Socrates, that education and instruction were ends in themselves. They believed that the study and instruction of the Law should be pursued without any other material object. Therefore there was a prohibition against taking any fixed sum in payment for the services as a teacher. "Do not make instruction a crown, to exalt yourself therewith, nor a spade, with which to dig;" meaning thereby, do not use your knowledge as a means of self-glorification, or as a means of livelihood. The care of the teachers was however provided for in general either by gifts or special aid. The Talmud says. "He who makes a present to a learned man does as good a deed as though he brought a first offering to the altar."

Maimonides in one of his commentaries writes: "We do not find anywhere that our wise men strove for earthly possessions. They did not collect money for the schools, for the judges and teachers. But we find among them at all times both the poorest and the richest." Most of these teachers, even if they were poor, could have had all the money they needed for the asking, but they preferred to support themselves by hard manual work.

The teachers of the very young children did receive pay for caring for them, and the pay of these teachers came from the general tax fund of the community. The schools were open to rich and poor alike, with the differ-

ence that the wealthier members of the community paid
a special school tax while the poor, who were exempt
from payment of all taxes, formed a class of free scholars.

IV. EDUCATION OF GIRLS.

Little is said in the Talmud about regularly organized
schools for girls.

The instruction they received, was mainly what may be
termed private instruction and consisted in the study of
the Bible.   That they must have been educated appears
from the wisdom with which the Jewish mothers exercised
their functions.   The Talmud says the parents must aid
their children in their studies, that is, the father and
mother.   The mothers often explained the lessons that
the teacher could not make their pupils understand, so
that though there were no schools their education was far
from neglected.   The education of girls was directed
rather to the training of their feelings rather than the
development of their understanding.   Girls were not to
become learned but rather intelligent mothers.   The Talmud asks, "Where will you find true religion?" and
answers by saying, "In a family where there is a good
mother."   In place of scientific training, the domestic
virtues were cultivated.   Household economy, dancing,
music, and Greek (the polite language of ancient days),
were the chief subjects of the education and curriculum
of girls.

There were also many learned women in those times.
Veruria wife of Rabbi Meir, was famous for her learning.
In the 12th century a Jewess delivered lectures on the
Talmud, and the daughter of Rabbi Meir wrote several
scientific treatises.

V. MANUAL TRAINING.

While the Rabbis had differing views as to the influence

of foreign culture, or as to the extent to which the education of women should be carried, in one respect they were unanimous, namely, in their respect for labor. It was axiomatic in their teaching that every boy should learn a trade. It must certainly seem strange to the reader of history to find in our nineteenth century a race that has honored labor as no other race has, accused of despising manual work, and as being desirous of living on the producers, rather than producing. Nearly all the great teachers of the Talmudic times were workmen. Hillel earned money enough to attend the Academy by wood-cutting. Rabbi Joshua was a blacksmith, others were tanners, carpenters, millers. They practiced what they taught and their teachings are finding appreciation at a time when manual training is coming to the front. "Labor was truly worship with them." Here are a few of the Talmudic sayings about work.

"Great is labor! it confers honor upon man, elevates the man who works, and brings support to the family."

"Choose any work and say not; 'I am a great man, a priest.'"

"The father who does not teach his children a trade, virtually brings him up to be a robber."

"The study of the law without occupation of labor will finally be interrupted and end in sin."

Work and study formed the principles of the educational system of the Talmudists. Study for the noblest purposes and not for money—work because it is man's duty. By this union was formed that intellectual force which we have said is a marked Hebrew characteristic.

There were no "middle ages" in Jewish history. While intellectual darkness prevailed in Christian lands, Hebrew Academies and schools for higher learning flourished in Toledo, Cordova, Narbonne, Padua and Rome.

The great Universities of France and Italy owe their existence to the Jewish doctors and philosophers who "contributed those elements of natural science and Greek philosophy which have increased in strength and volume in our modern academic life."

The school is in modern days still dear to the Hebrew. Parents feel it a sacred duty to have their children well educated and Jewish pupils are among the brightest in the schools and colleges of the world. In works of philanthropy and charity, the Hebrews are ever foremost and no movement of the advance guard "of educational workers finds more supporters than among that race truly styled the people of the Book."